Moon Base Beta

Written by Ciaran Murtagh

Illustrated by Kevin Hopgood

Collins

Since he was eight years old, Brian Claxon had dreamt of walking on the Moon. He remembered sitting in his grandad's back garden and staring up at the night sky in wonder. His grandad knew the names of all the stars and, as he pointed them out, Brian decided that one day he would go to the Moon.

His grandad chuckled when Brian told him his plan.

"Don't be daft, Brian," he said. "People like us don't go to the Moon!"

Brian didn't listen. He knew that if you worked hard enough, anybody – even Brian Claxon – could walk on the Moon.

Which is why, as Brian sat in the Space Port waiting for his name to be called, he allowed himself a little smile. Brian was about to become an astronaut.

Brian looked at the other astronauts waiting to leave. He couldn't believe he was in the same room as them, let alone that he was about to launch into space on the same shuttle.

There was Clint Lockjaw, hero of the mission to Jupiter, Marina Firmstride, the first woman on Mars, and Jessie Clench, the first astronaut to explore a black hole and live to tell the tale. They were some of the bravest people in the galaxy and they were about to become his shipmates.

They were all going to Moon Base Beta. The base was a brand-new, high-tech research facility built right on the Moon's surface. Brian couldn't wait to be part of the action.

Just then, a woman in a bright green spacesuit marched into the holding area and called the astronauts to attention.

"I am Officer Hubble," she announced. "Commanding officer of your mission to Moon Base Beta. I shall be coordinating things from down here. Now listen carefully – you all have a very important part to play, if your mission is going to be a success."

She looked at each of the astronauts in turn.

"Clint, you are the mission commander. Whilst on base, you're going to be plotting a new route to Mars avoiding asteroid belts. Jessie, your mission is to find a way to grow sustainable plants in zero gravity. Marina, you're up there to mine minerals, and Brian –"

Brian looked up expectantly.

"You're there to keep everything clean and tidy."

Clint chuckled. Brian didn't care. Everywhere needed someone to tidy up, even a moon base, and Brian was proud to do the job.

Officer Hubble turned and led the astronauts through a pair of silver doors.

"Let's get you kitted out," she said. "Your shuttle leaves in 30 minutes."

In the next room, smart-looking spacesuits hung off pegs. Each had the name of an astronaut stitched on the back. Clint, Jessie and Marina all had silver spacesuits; Brian's was brown.

"Can't I have a silver one too?" asked Brian.

Clint chuckled again.

"Only proper astronauts get proper spacesuits," he sneered. "You're just a space cleaner."

Things only got worse when Officer Hubble opened up a cupboard full of cool-looking space gadgets. Clint got a touch-screen notepad, Jessie a pair of power gloves covered in buttons, and Marina a hammer that doubled up as a laser saw. Brian got a mop.

"What's this?" asked Brian.

"An Intergalactic Space Mop," said Officer Hubble.

Clint chuckled again. Brian had a feeling he and Clint were not going to get along.

In the shuttle, the other astronauts took seats near the front. They all had important jobs to do and started checking computer readouts. Jessie flashed Brian a smile as she worked.

"Good to have you on board," she said.

Brian smiled back; at least someone wanted him there.

Clint flicked a switch
and the shuttle's rockets
rumbled into life.
Brian's whole seat
began to wobble.
He gulped nervously.

"Strap in, space
cleaner," barked Clint.
"And try not to get
space sick!"

The countdown began.

Ten ... nine ... eight ...

Suddenly, Brian wasn't
sure he wanted to go to
the Moon, after all.

Seven ... six ...
five ... four ...

But it was too late now.

Three ... two ... one!

They were off.
The shuttle roared into
the sky.

The journey to the Moon took longer than Brian
thought it would.

Clint turned on the artificial gravity generator whilst
the other astronauts kept an eye on their screens and
adjusted their controls.

Brian decided it would be a good time to examine his space mop a little more closely. It was clear that this was no ordinary mop: it was covered in buttons and switches. He had no idea what they did.

Brian pushed a blue button and a dollop of cleaning fluid splurted out of a hidden nozzle. It splatted Clint on the back of the neck.

"Watch it, space cleaner!" snarled Clint.

Brian shrank a little into his seat and gave Clint an apologetic smile.

Brian decided to try a different button. He pushed the big green one. A tube appeared and the space mop made a terrific noise. Brian had pressed the vacuum button. Brian dropped the mop in shock and watched in horror as it roared around the cabin, pinging off the walls.

"Catch it before it does any damage," called Clint, who was trying to concentrate on flying the ship.

Marina leapt out of her seat and grabbed the handle as it flew past. She fumbled with the buttons until the space mop powered down.

She gave the mop back to Brian with a wink.

"Who knew I'd be saving us from a runaway space mop today?" she said.

Clint turned and gave Brian a fierce stare.

"Sit there and don't touch anything until we land.
Do you understand?"

Brian nodded as he put the space mop under
his seat. His mission had not got off to a good start.

A couple of hours later, they were landing on the Moon. Brian had to pinch himself to check he wasn't dreaming, as he stared through the window in awe.

Moon Base Beta was even more spectacular than he'd imagined. Its glass biosphere glinted in the half-light. It looked like a massive greenhouse!

Brian couldn't believe he was about to call this wonderful place home.

"Helmets on," ordered Clint. "We won't have oxygen until I activate the filtration system."

As they made their way inside the base, Brian struggled to take it all in.

Everything about Moon Base Beta seemed fresh and new. It was packed with equipment and each astronaut had a designated work space. There was a gleaming office for Clint, and Jessie had an area that looked like a cross between a garden centre and a living room. On the other side of the base, Marina had a science lab covered in charts and full of gleaming silver tools.

At the heart of everything was a kitchen, and a lounge with the comfiest-looking sofa Brian had ever seen.

Clint flicked a switch, and Brian heard the filtration system whirr into action.

Clint took off his helmet.

"OK, everybody," he said. "It's safe."

The crew took off their helmets and settled in. There was just one thing bothering Brian.

"Erm, Clint," he said. "Where can I put my things?"

"Out back, space cleaner," snapped Clint. He pointed to a door Brian hadn't noticed, hidden at the back of the kitchen.

Brian went to see. He found himself in what he thought was a storage cupboard. Brian moved a big box to one side to reveal a bed. It wasn't what he was expecting.

"Home sweet home," he said to himself, as he tried to make himself comfortable.

Later that evening, after dinner, Jessie and Marina suggested that Brian could make the comfy lounge his base if he wanted. Clint was having none of it. Brian had his space and they had theirs.

Over the next few days, Brian tried to make
the best of his situation. He was still an astronaut and
he was still on the Moon – that was something to be
proud of. And as the other astronauts got on with
their work, Brian got on with his.

Brian's job was to keep the Moon Base tidy and, with all of the moondust and experimentation going on, there was a lot of work to do. Luckily, Brian had his space mop. He'd spent time figuring out what all the buttons did and now he was a bit of an expert.

It really was a remarkable tool. The space mop could clean just about anything. Colourful buttons shot out cleaning fluid, dusters, plungers and just about anything else a space cleaner might need!

Brian's jobs included keeping everything neat and tidy, making meals, getting rid of rubbish and – the job he hated most of all – emptying the hydro toilet.

It was very stinky and involved a dangerous walk on the Moon's surface to manually release the hatch. Luckily, he had found a special face mask and oxygen pump amongst the cleaning supplies that made things a little better. He would pop on the mask and get to work with nice clean fresh air filling his nostrils.

One evening, whilst he was outside emptying the hydro toilet, disaster struck. It all started when a small rock landed at Brian's feet. Where had that come from? Brian looked up to the sky as another rock landed, then another and another.

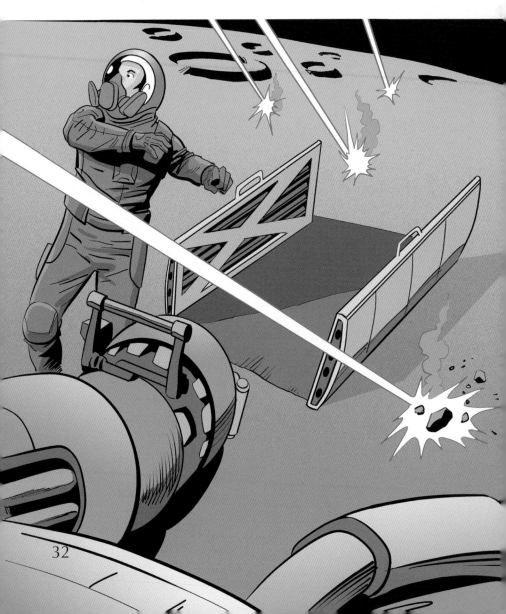

Suddenly, Brian's communication device burst into life. It was Officer Hubble.

"We're picking up an asteroid strike! Everybody, take cover!"

Everyone else was safely inside the Moon Base, but Brian needed to find somewhere to hide – fast!

Brian dodged the asteroid shower. The tiny rocks fell like hailstones, as he searched for somewhere to hide.

In the end, he opened the stinky hydro toilet chute and jumped inside, pulling the lid closed.

Brian listened to the asteroids rain down all around and, when he was sure the danger had passed, he clambered out. His suit was covered in muck, but at least he was alive.

Brian made his way back to the Moon Base. He couldn't wait to tell the others what had just happened. As he made his way inside, he took off his face mask, but quickly put it back on again – he couldn't breathe. Something wasn't right.

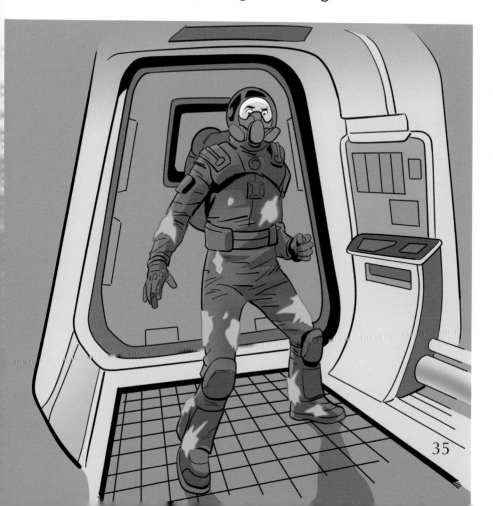

One look around the base confirmed Brian's suspicions. Clint was in his office slumped over his desk. Brian ran over and tried to wake him up, but he was unconscious. Marina and Jessie were both slumped at their workstations too. This wasn't good. This wasn't good at all.

He ran to the big computer and pushed the buttons he'd seen Clint press whenever he wanted to contact Officer Hubble.

Suddenly, her face filled the screen.

"Brian? What's going on? Is everything OK?"

Words tumbled out of Brian like moon rocks.

"No! Everything is not OK!" he said.

"Something's happened! Everyone's unconscious."

Officer Hubble tapped some keys on her keypad.

"There's a problem with the oxygen supply," she said. "It must have been damaged in the asteroid storm."

"You'll have to fix it," said Officer Hubble.

"Me!?" said Brian. "I'm just the space cleaner!"

"They need air *now*!" said Officer Hubble.
"You've got this, Brian!"

Brian raced back outside to see if he could find
the problem. It didn't take him long to spot it. The air
unit was jammed by a large asteroid. Brian reported
back to Officer Hubble.

"You have to unblock it!" she said.

"But I don't know how!" spluttered Brian.

"There must be a way, Brian," said Officer Hubble. "They're all relying on you!"

The air unit was on the top of the Moon Base, and the asteroid was stopping it sucking in any air at all. Brian tried to reach the asteroid, but it was too high. Next, he tried to dislodge it with a moon rock, but the rock just pinged off the asteroid and disappeared into space.

Nothing was working! If only he had a cool gadget like the other astronauts. But then Brian realised – he did.

He ran and fetched his space mop.

"Come on, space mop!" he said. "Don't let me down!"

Brian pressed a button and the space mop extended.

"Perfect for those hard-to-reach places," he said.

Then he pressed the big green button and
the vacuum whirred into life. Brian aimed the space
mop at the asteroid.

"You can do this, Brian," he said quietly to himself,
as he turned the dial to maximum.

The powerful suction latched onto the asteroid
and, with one massive heave, Brian yanked it clear of
the filtration system.

"Thank you, space mop," he said, as he raced
back inside.

Brian took off his mask and tested the air.
Oxygen was flowing again and, in his office, Clint was
starting to stir.

"What happened?" he mumbled. "I don't feel
so good."

"You lost some air in here," explained Brian.
"But you'll be fine after a little lie-down."

Marina and Jessie were also starting to come round.
Once he'd tucked Clint into bed, Brian helped them get
some rest too.

Officer Hubble's voice crackled through the communicator.

"Well done, Brian, you saved them all!"

"With a little help from my space mop," said Brian proudly.

Over the next few days, Brian patiently nursed his fellow astronauts back to health, and soon they were as right as rain. Clint thanked Brian for his bravery and never called him "space cleaner" again. Brian was even allowed to make the lounge his home.

One evening, a few days after the asteroid strike, Officer Hubble summoned everybody into the living quarters. Her face filled the communication screen. She was holding a shiny silver spacesuit, and Brian's name was stitched across the back.

"This will be waiting for you when you get back, Brian," she announced. "And a new name has been added to our long list of heroes. Joining Clint Lockjaw, hero of the mission to Jupiter, Marina Firmstride, the first woman on Mars, and Jessie Clench, the astronaut who explored a black hole and lived to tell the tale, is Brian Claxon, proud protector of Moon Base Beta."

Brian had never been happier, and as he listened to the applause ring out from his fellow astronauts, he looked out to the stars and thought of his grandad. He hoped that wherever his grandad was now, he felt just as proud as he did.

An interview with Clint

As commander of a mission to space, I thought I knew all there was to know about heroes. Then I met Brian Claxon.

I thought he was nothing more than a space cleaner, someone to tidy my mess and keep out of my way. I couldn't have been more wrong. If it weren't for Brian and his quick thinking, I wouldn't be here now.

Brian and his space mop saved my life. His quick thinking and courage are a testament to us all and I'm proud to call him a friend.

I now know that heroes come in all shapes and sizes and some of them carry a space mop.

Thanks, Brian, I'll never leave planet Earth without you again!

Ideas for reading

Written by Gill Matthews
Primary Literacy Consultant

Reading objectives:

- ask questions to improve understanding of a text
- draw inferences such as inferring characters' feelings, thoughts and motives from their actions, and justify inferences with evidence
- identify how language, structure and presentation contribute to meaning

Spoken language objectives:

- articulate and justify answers, arguments and opinions
- participate in discussions, presentations, performances, role play, improvisations and debates

Curriculum links: Design and technology – Design

Interest words: sneered, barked, snarled

Build a context for reading

- Ask children to look closely at the front cover illustration and to read the title. Encourage them to predict who the character is, what he's holding and where he is.
- Read the back cover blurb. Focus on the second sentence. Ask the children if they think this is a fair thing to say. Encourage them to justify their responses with reasons.
- Ask the children what they think *to prove his worth* means and how Brian will do this.

Understand and apply reading strategies

- Read pp2–3 aloud to the children. Ask how they feel about what Brian's grandad said, that people like them couldn't go to the Moon. Explore children's reactions to the final sentence.
- Read pp4–7 aloud. Ask children how they think Brian is feeling. Reread the final paragraph on p7. Ask children to explain what it shows about Clint and Brian.